PIANO SOLO

WORSHIP WITHOUT WORDS

Y0-IWE-071

Piano Arrangements for Blended Worship by Ken Medema

CONTENTS

ISBN 0-634-09999-X

HAL•LEONARD® CORPORATION

7777 W. BLUEMOUND RD. P.O.BOX 13819 MILWAUKEE, WI 53213

Visit Hal Leonard Online at
www.halleonard.com

AS THE DEER

Words and Music by
MARTIN NYSTROM
Arranged by Ken Medema

Moderately slow, expressively

cresc. poco a poco
f

mf

3
(♩ = ♩)
5
M4
8va
middle
D
8va
Both
middle
f

mp
mf
mp

DOWN TO THE RIVER TO PRAY

Traditional
Arranged by Ken Medema

Moderately

* *Quote from "Down by the Riverside" (Traditional Spiritual)*

5 3 2 1

f
dim.
mf

mf

mp

I COULD SING OF YOUR LOVE FOREVER

(Based on "Morning" by Edvard Grieg)

Words and Music by
MARTIN SMITH
Arranged by Ken Medema

Flowing, in a moderate four

mf

sim.

f

cresc.
ff
dim.
mf
cresc.
ff
dim.
mf

mp
cresc.
mf

mp
8va
(8va)
loco

LORD, LISTEN TO YOUR CHILDREN PRAYING

Words and Music by
KEN MEDEMA
Arranged by Ken Medema

Moderate Gospel feel

8vb
loco
f

8vb
loco
mf
8vb
loco
mp

f
dim.
mf

mf
8vb
loco
5 1
dim.
L.H.
8vb

I WILL CALL UPON THE LORD

(with "A Little Something in C")

Words and Music by
MICHAEL O'SHIELDS
Arranged by Ken Medema

A LITTLE SOMETHING IN C
By KEN MEDEMA

1 2 4 1
f

mf
5
mp
cresc. poco a poco
f
ff

mf
f
mf
cresc.
f

mf
cresc. poco a poco
8vb
loco
ff
8va
(8va)
loco
5
5

LEANING ON THE EVERLASTING ARMS

(with "O Rest in the Lord" from *Elijah*)

Words by ELISHA A. HOFFMAN
Music by ANTHONY J. SHOWALTER
Arranged by Ken Medema

mp

mf
mf
f
mf
dim.
mp

O REST IN THE LORD
By FELIX MENDELSSOHN

mf
f
mf

mp
rit.

LET ALL MORTAL FLESH KEEP SILENCE

(with "When I Survey the Wondrous Cross")

Words from the Liturgy of ST. JAMES
17th Century French Carol
Arranged by Ken Medema

WHEN I SURVEY THE WONDROUS CROSS
Words by ISAAC WATTS
Music based on Plainsong

8va
loco
8va

loco
dim. poco a poco
8vb

LORD, I LIFT YOUR NAME ON HIGH

Words and Music by
RICK FOUNDS
Arranged by Ken Medema

To Coda

2 1 2

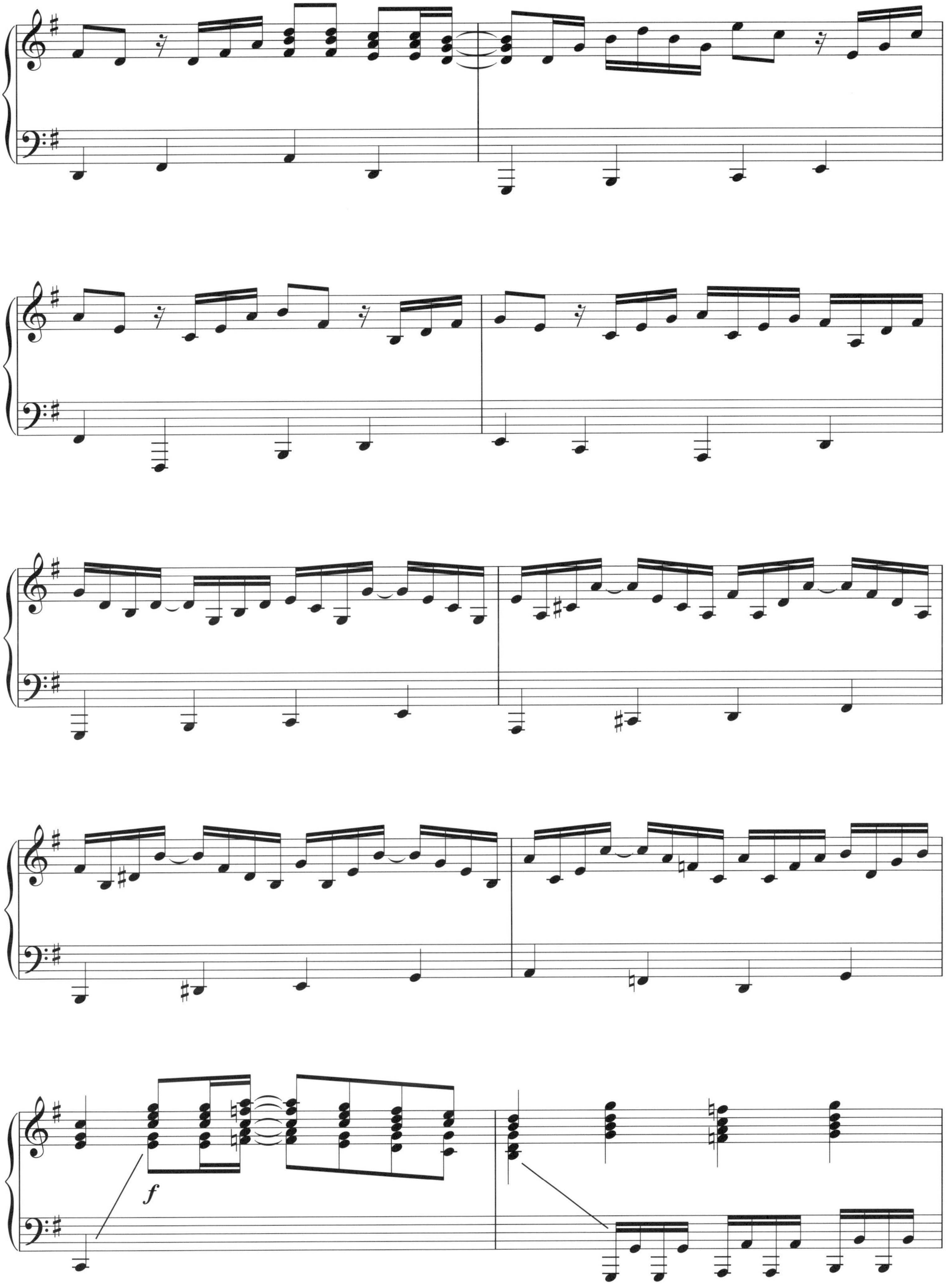

dim.
mf
dim.

D.S. al Coda
CODA
2
gradually building to end
2
2
2
2
8va
loco

OPEN THE EYES OF MY HEART

Words and Music by
PAUL BALOCHE
Arranged by Ken Medema

Steadily, not too fast

f
mp

cresc.
f
mp
f
mf

dim.
mf
dim. e rit.
8va

YOU ARE MY ALL IN ALL

By DENNIS JERNIGAN
Arranged by Ken Medema

cresc.
f

dim.
mf
bring out melody
f

mf

dim. e rit.
8vb